True Stories of Pat & Nell

The Love Affair of the Century

*'And I'd Choose You,
In a Hundred Lifetimes,
In a Hundred Worlds,
In any Version of Reality,
I'd find you and
I'd Choose You.'*

The Chaos of Stars

True Stories of Pat & Nell

The Love Affair of the Century

Written by: Nellie Garbitt

Edited by Tiffanee J.A. Griffiths

Published by Nellie Garbitt
2017

Copyright

True Stories of Pat and Nell; The Love Affair of the Century

Moberly Lake, Peace River Region, British Columbia, Canada

Copyright © 2017 by Nellie Garbitt

All rights reserved. This book or any portion thereof may not be reproduced or used in any manner whatsoever without the express written permission of the publisher except for the use of brief quotations in a book review or scholarly journal.

First Printing: 2017. Second Edition: 2018

ISBN 978-1-365-82384-8

Nellie Garbitt
Box 284
Moberly Lake British Columbia, Canada. V0C1X0

Email: nellie@moberlylake.net PH:250.788.4205

Dedication

This Book is dedicated to my children, Jordon (Buckskin), Clayton (Rawhide), Rosalee (Chick-a-Dee), Willow, and my grandchildren; Mariah and Kierra.
Also, this book is dedicated to Pat's children Patsy, Wayne (Bimbo), Nick (Smokey), Darrell (Porky), Sandra, Warren (Poco) and Jackie, and their children.
I would like to do a special dedication, and Thank You, to God our Father, and Jesus Christ our Savior, who carefully planned and blessed the union of Pat and Nellie Garbitt. Also, to my husband and other half, Pat Garbitt, who crossed over to the other side of the veil on March 25, 1993.

Table of Contents

Table of Contents

The Love Affair of the Century i
The Chaos of Stars iii
True Stories of Pat & Nell v
Copyright vi
Dedication ix
From the Author xvii
Preface xx
Words from Heaven xxii
   To Last a Lifetime xxii
Pat's mom's Vision 3
Pat's History 5
Nell's History 11
The Day I met Pat 13
Pat and I Bathing 17
   In the Love of the Holy Spirit 17
Soul Mates 19
Pat's Reoccurring Dream 21
Pat's Energy 23
Caught in a Precious Moment 27

The Piano	29
A Magic Moment	31
The Explosion	33
Signs of Pat's oncoming Death	35
Pat's Sister's Gift	37
From the other side of the Veil	37
The Night the Northern Lights	39
Came to see me	39
Flowers from Heaven	43
The Morning Jesus Spoke to me	47
The 1st Time I was shown	49
A little bit of Heaven	49
The 2nd time I was shown Heaven	53
Angels wake me to Pray	55
Four things told to me by God	57
My Daughter Willow's Birth	61
Foretold by an Angel	61
Eagle Feathers	62
An Angel Sent to Us	65
What I learned	69
From Handicapped People	69
My Dreams of Pat	71
We are One	72

Answer to Prayer 72
Pat's Extraordinary Experiences 75
Nell's Extraordinary Experiences 79
Cleansed our Home of all Evil 85
My Testimony 87
    Of a Priesthood Blessing 87
Seeing 11:11 89
Four Leaf Clovers 91
Pat Appeared 93
    My last Words to Pat 93
    To Hear Pat's Voice Again 94
To Face your Fears 97
My Reiki Treatment 99
Pat's Funeral Announcement 103
A Whisper from God 105
References 106
Glossary 107

From the Author

  This book is filled with true stories, of experiences that happened to Pat and I. These stories are being told to let our children know, that when things get tough, there really is help out there that we cannot see. Also, to let everyone know, that miracles of many different types do happen. These stories are a Testimony that God our Father lives, and he loves us more than we can comprehend. That Jesus Christ is truly the Son of God and our Savior, and came to this earth, and died for our sins to give us life in the world to come, and is as close as your right ear. This is also a Testimony that the Holy Spirit is with us to help us every moment of our life.

  Prayer really works, and the stories in this book are proof of that.

  These stories are true and are written with hopes that they bring Inspiration and Blessings to each and every one who reads them.

Preface

There were people that used to call Pat and I "The Love Affair of the Century", so this is where the title of this book comes from. I always wanted to receive first hand, the gifts and experiences I would hear coming from Pastor's, Medicine Men/Women, and different gifted people. I listened to the stories, and prayed, I read everything about the subject that I could. When Pat died, everything in my life changed. Many things happened, some of which are recorded here.

This book is made up of a series of true stories. Most of them are short, some before and some after Pat's death, but all worth recording and passing on. It is my hope that they may touch your heart in some way. The Purpose of recording and passing these stories on to my children and the rest of the world is my way of declaring the truth that there is a living God our Father, a Living son Jesus Christ our Savior, and the precious Holy Spirit, that are all here to help us through the schooling of Life.

It is my hope that you can know that you are in the right place, at the right time in your journey, even if it doesn't feel like it at the time. God Bless each and every one of you that take the time to read these stories through, and may they help you to realize, that all things are possible.

Words from Heaven

To Last a Lifetime

God has Blessed me with a lifelong friend, who is very spiritually gifted. After Pat crossed over to the other side of the veil, these are the words that he told her to give to me,

"Nell, you are my Pride and Joy,
Our children are the love we share
In their eyes I see you and me…
Dancing the Dance of Love
Dear God I want them to realize the
Special qualities they carry
The strength of our Love
Is running in their veins…
This is life energy beyond measure…….
They were conceived with so much love
Ask them all to Remember Me and you Nell
And all the love we put in their Veins.
They need only to feel the strength of the flow
Our life force in theirs
Our Love is always with them
They are never alone…
We are all One…..
As one we walk this earth together
We are Proud and Strong in our Heart Songs"

Pat's mom's Vision

Martha Garbitt, Pat's mother, was very gifted and a Prophetess. As she lay dying in her hospital bed, she told Pat that he was going to be alright. "Don't worry my boy," she said, "You will be happy again. I have seen it. You are going to meet a girl that is sweet and kind, and is really going to love you. You will love her so much. She will treat you really good. You will be very happy with her." Pat's mom continued to say "I see three children with you and her, two boys and a girl. But after that, alcohol will kill you."

This, word for word, is exactly what happened.

Pat was born February 16, 1928 in Jackfish Lake, outside of Chetwynd, British Columbia, Canada. His dad was Scotch and his mother was full blooded Saulteau Indian.

I was born January 31, 1953 in Bielen, Holland. Both of my parents were Dutch.

When Pat and I met, he was 53 years old and I was 28. He was born in 1928, and I in 1953, and he always laughed and said the coincidence was 'Meant to be.'

The twenty-five years between us was never felt by him, nor did I, and I believe we were Soul Mates of the real kind, and had to meet in this lifetime no matter what age.

Clayton, Rosalee, Jordon

Garbitt

Pat's History

Pat's mother had said, during the Louis Riel Rebellion, a band of Saulteau Indians in Manitoba, were starving because all of the buffalo herds were destroyed. The Indians were given food in rations by the government agents. Our Saulteau Tribe sent out Pat's Grandfather (his mother's dad), and his brother to get food from the Indian Agent. The Indian Agent refused to give them anything so they killed him. They gathered up the food and they ran. They loaded up their families and took what they could, and left on foot.

Pat's Grandfather had a vision. They 'Must travel West, across the Prairies', and said that if he could find a lake that lay East and West with two mountains, twin peaks that formed the shape of a woman's breast at the western end, they would find peace and sanctuary there.

The journey took thirteen years from Manitoba to Moberly Lake, while all this time they were being hunted by the North West Mounted Police. During their walk across the Prairies, the police almost caught them. Pat's Grandfather prayed, and a heavy fog came down that allowed them to get away.

Pat's mother was born on the journey, at Duck Lake Alberta. Her name was Martine

Saulteau, later to be called Martha Desjarlais. After thirteen years with some of their people dying along the way, they reached Progress, British Columbia, a settlement west of Dawson Creek. There, Pat's Grandfather finally saw the Twin Peak Mountains shown to him in his vision.

They travelled the rest of the way to the Twin Peaks. When they arrived there, a baby fell off a horse a rolled down a mountain and was killed. They got frightened and thought that this was a sign to move on from there. They could see Moberly Lake was the place of safety to live. From that time on that's where they stayed.

Pat's father, Harry Garbitt, came from Aberdeen, Scotland at the age of sixteen. He arrived in old Fort St. John in 1895. Harry bought furs, guided, trapped, hauled mail and ran a Trading Post in Moberly Lake. Harry was very well known and spoke Cree as easily as English. He met Martha Desjarlais, Pat's mom, in Moberly Lake who already had a son named Fred at the time. Harry already had a son named Slim, and together the two of them eventually had Gertie, Maryanne, Angus and Pat.

Pat was born in a small cabin a few miles from Chetwynd, in a place called Jackfish Lake. The Catholic Church came around and gathered all the Native children to educate them. They took them to

Residential School in Gruard, Alberta. They took Gertie and Maryanne, Pat was too little, but Angus (only four years old) wanted to go so bad because he was so close to the girls, he put up such a fuss they said he would be just fine to go, so they took him as well. As soon as they got there, Angus was separated away from Gertie and Maryanne because the girls and the boys were kept in separate dorms. He stood at the fence crying for his sisters every day until he died. They allowed him to die of fear and loneliness, while everyone at home thought he was fine.

Pat grew up strong, smart and very handsome. He was close to his mom, dad and sisters. His personality was huge and attracted people to him from a young age. He had a very good sense of humor, making people laugh around him wherever he went. Girls threw themselves at him right from a very young age as well. So badly that it affected his learning at school and was finally asked to leave because of it… at about grade 6.

So he had to start working. As he grew older he was determined to be self-taught and do everything just as good as, or better than anyone else. He caught on fast and always had the best paying jobs when there was work.

People were very prejudice then, and it was not always easy to land the jobs because of this.

When the Bennett Dam first started, there were men brought in from all over the world. Pat walked from Moberly Lake all the way to the Bennett Dam to try and get hired on. They said no. He went back to Moberly, but his family was having a hard time so he walked all the way back up to the Dam and asked again. They said no, again. So he told them he was going to sit in their office until they hired him. He was hired the next day.

Prejudice was something that was around all the time in those days. Pat would continually fight for the Native People and their Rights. He was in many fights, protecting others. People grew to respect him in every town he went to. Soon he was very well known in the white man's world as well as the Native, and always fighting for Native rights, proving to the white people that the natives were just as good, if not better than many of them.

Wherever he went, the white women, as well as native women continued to throw themselves at his feet. Not only was he strong and handsome, but he was respectful, funny, smart, and had more charisma than anyone I have ever seen.

Pat loved women too. They threw themselves at him throughout his whole life. You just couldn't help but understand this because of the man he was. I certainly didn't blame them. He was every woman's dream, and all the men wanted to be like him. It was like walking with a movie star. People were attracted to him wherever he went.

He was approached to go to Hollywood to become a star. He was also approached to run as the Peace River MLA in Government, to run for Chief at Two First Nations, and Grande Chief for multiple First Nations at Treaty Section 8. He did attend the meetings at Treaty 8 with all the Chief's when they would gather, whenever he was asked to.

Our People wanted him to represent them but Pat did not want to be in the Public's eye. His work with his people was at a different level. He would love the unloved, take people in and care for the poor and down-hearted for as long as they chose, or needed to stay with him. Some stayed two days, some two weeks, and some, two years.

Pat had a first marriage, with Gladys Girou. They had seven beautiful children. They always struggled with their relationship, and finally ended it.

I met Pat a couple of years after he ended their relationship. We maintained a friendship with her and his first children throughout our life together.

Pat's 1st family

Nell's History

On the night of January 31, 1953, the dikes broke in Holland and 1,500 people were killed. This was the night I was born, in a town called Bielen, Holland.

My mother's name was Nellie Hoekzema, and my dad's name was Jacobus (Bob) Hoekzema

My mother was running around the table in labor giving birth to me in absolute terror as the storm raged and the dikes broke. I was born very quickly, only 5lbs. My mother ended up with a blood clot in her leg and was taken to the hospital where she spent six weeks laying on her back to get rid of the clot. Then, she developed Thrombosis that she fought with for the rest of her life.

We moved to Canada when I was 2 ½ years old. We came by ship landing in Halifax, and took the train to Vancouver where we settled until I was 9 years old. My mom and dad had so many troubles when they got here that they split up. My mother then married Jan Haagsman. He moved us north to a small town called Hudson's Hope, where they raised eight children, me being one of them.

We were raised very strict, and when we were old enough to quit school Dad (Jan) took us out to work at home. He got six sections of land near Chinaman Lake so we moved there. We cleared land, farmed and raised cattle, and there was a saw mill where the boys worked at too. We were not allowed to leave the farm and go out on a date so it was a very lonely time for me. I developed epilepsy from being what I may call 'Caged'. I learned many good things while on the farm that would help me in the years to come, one of them being how to work, hard.

When I was 26, Dad and I got into a fight and he sent me to town at 3:00am and -30 below Celsius. He thought I would come back because I had nowhere to go after spending so many years on the farm, but I was free. Like letting a bird out of its cage, and I didn't return until Pat and I were married and had our first son, Jordon.

Pat and Nell's Parents

Nellie and Bob Hoekzema./ Harry Garbitt and Martha Desjarlais

The Day I met Pat

Being in the Right Place, at the Right Time, in Eternity.

I had proof of this, and it seems huge. It isn't often any one of us can say that. What I have had with Pat in this lifetime, is what few people are lucky enough to find, and was given to us by God himself. Proof that God does indeed answer prayers, word for word in His own time. God does not forget one word of what you have prayed, here is proof to this.

When I spent all those years on the farm, lonely, I would pray to God each night and talk to him about how I was going to meet my husband. I was twenty-six years old and it seemed impossible because of being confined to stay on the farm and not allowed to date.

I would talk to God about what I desired and my visualization of a tall, handsome man that was dark skinned, loved God, and horses.

I would say to God, "If I meet the right man for me, as a sign, please have him say this to me as soon as we meet; I want to spend my life with you", and for him to want to marry me as soon as he sees me, that would be his sign.

Three days before I met Pat, I prayed with all my heart and asked God to forgive me of the sins I was doing, and gave myself to God and said "I will do whatever you want me to do." Then, I met Pat. As big as life, he was sitting in the bar, in Hudson's Hope surrounded by people like he always was. He looked handsome, and was very funny.

As soon as he saw me he said to his son (from his first marriage) "I am going to marry her if I can get her."

My girlfriend Arlene and I sat with him and his table full of people. He kept asking Arlene in Cree language questions about me. Then I wanted to leave, this was only the second time I had ever been in a bar, being shy and just off the farm, I was not so used to people. He asked where we would be that night, we told him we were going to the Casino night at the Town Hall, he said he would meet us there, and we departed.

Arlene and I arrived at the Town Hall, and got seated at our table when this man comes up, who we hardly knew, and said "Nellie, there is someone here you have to meet," he continued "You have to spend your life with him." I replied with "Who are you talking about?"

"Pat Garbitt." He said.

I smiled and said I had met him that afternoon at the bar. The man was happy, and left.

Pat found our table and sat down; he took my hands in his. He looked me in the eyes and said "I want to spend my Life with you." We stayed together from that moment on. A few days later he took me out to his land on the other side of Moberly Lake. We entered his little log cabin where he went straight to the ceiling in the corner. He took down a small blue leather sack, and took out a diamond ring, he took my hands in his and asked,

"Will you marry me?" Of course, I said yes.

∙∙∙

We really did have a Fairy Tale marriage. So deeply in love, always travelling together, always laughing, and we had three of the most beautiful children God could have ever Blessed us with. Just like his mom told him before she died; 'You will have two boys, and a girl, and you will be very happy together.' *see Pat's Mom's Vision

Pat and I Bathing
In the Love of the Holy Spirit

When Pat and I first got together, we lived on Beryl Prairie road, just outside of Hudson's Hope, BC.

For the first three months, I would wake up during the night and I would feel so much love in the room surrounding Pat and I. It was so strong that it is hard to describe how it felt. First, I wondered if it was coming from Pat, then when I realized he was sound asleep, I knew it was not coming from him. Then I thought... is it me? But it was moving through me and around me and filling the room. It was very powerful, yet gentle and warm. It felt like it was coming out of me as well as going through me, and it would put me back to sleep. This happened many nights when we first found each other.

It was years later when I was much older, did I learn that it really was the Holy Spirit bathing us in his Love, and Blessing our Union.

This experience I think of many times, and I am so grateful.

Soul Mates

What would I call this story?

"Divine Love", or "Twin Flames", "The Night our Spirits sealed us Together", I chose "Soul Mates" but all are worth mentioning to define this tale.

One night, while Pat and I were lying in bed together, about one week before he passed away, he was holding me close to him and we were just loving each other's closeness. His face was tucked in my neck when, something happened.

All of a sudden, I was in Pat's spirit, and he was in my spirit. I didn't want to say anything or move, for fear it would stop. I was literally inside of him, feeling him, being him, seeing through him, and seeing the color of his spirit. The same was happening to him as he was inside of me, seeing through me, feeling me, being me, and seeing the color of my spirit.

I said to him, very softly, "Is this happening to you too?"

All he said was "We are one."

Our spirits were loving each other so much that we were like one Being. It was unbelievable. Something I did not know was possible of ever happening in this world.

We did not even speak of this to each other or to anyone else in the days that followed, but it was only a few days and then, he was gone.

I believe with all my heart that Pat and I have been sealed together for here and eternity. We really are "Soul Mates."

Pat's Reoccurring Dream

Right after Pat and I got together, he woke up one morning and said "I had that dream again." I asked "What dream?" He replied "I always have this dream of a beautiful place where the grass is greener than here and has the most beautiful meadows, lakes and hills. All the horses I have owned in my life that have died are there. Everything is more beautiful there."

A few weeks later he woke up in the morning and said the same thing; that he had that dream again. It happened again, only this time he said "I had that dream again. This time in the dream, I was riding a black stallion and you were with me, riding a white stallion.

That was the last time he had that dream.

Pat's Energy

Pat had a huge presence and energy. Wherever he went, people were drawn to him like he was a huge magnet. When we would walk down streets of different towns, I felt as though I were walking with a movie star because of the energy that surrounded him. Our energies together made this stronger. People would stop us on the street, or come and sit with us in public places. Pat took this as normal and would talk and visit with whoever came around us. He took me everywhere. He loved his people and they adored him. He had a kind heart, and took time for everyone.

He loved the mountains the most. He loved the land, and loved living the way the Natives lived in the days of old. He always helped the lowly people. He loved them and taught me how to love. He always picked up homeless people, or people who were down-and-out, and brought them home to stay with us. We did have guest cabins Pat had built to accommodate these people. Some of them would stay for a few days, some a few months, and some a few years.

We lived on Pat's ¾ section of land that was 20 miles in the bush. He built a beautiful log house for us to raise our family in. Here, it was like a world all it's own. It seemed there was no world outside of our Home there. When we would go to bed, we both loved to be held by each other, so we would take turns. He would hold me first, then when we turned around, I would hold him. It would feel just like magic when we turned and I would lie against him and hold him. It would feel like all the cares in the whole world would be drawn out through my stomach and into him. All my cares would leave me. It would feel like magic.

People loved coming and staying there. I am sure over the years we had no less than fifty people come and stay there for a time to get their feet back on the ground. We had no power or running water. We lived off the land as much as we could. We raised our children there until Pat passed away.

I grew up with the land, working it, growing from it, so when Pat taught me the native way of living off the land, it was easy for me to adapt to this life.

Pat had many different opportunities offered to him through his life, but turned them all down because of his love for living off the land and his love for his people.

One time he was asked to go to Hollywood to become a Movie Star.

Another time he was asked to run as the MLA for the Peace River Region.

He was asked to become Chief of two different Nations.

He turned these down because I believe he was to teach us all how to love one another and how to love the unloved.

Caught in a Precious Moment

When Pat and I first moved in together, we lived in a cabin he had built for himself before I met him. It was small, so when we had our second son, he decided to build us a bigger home.

He built a beautiful log house with the help of dear friends. It only took six months to build and turned out very beautiful. Once we moved in, Pat really wanted to have a baby girl, so I agreed.

One night as we were all going to bed, I happened to overhear Pat and the boys in their room. I tip-toed over to the door and peeked in. They all had their hands folded and heads bowed in prayer. Pat was praying out loud saying "Please God, help mommy to have a baby girl, and please could she look just like mommy."

We had been trying for quite a few months, but after that prayer, I became pregnant that next month, with a little girl. Pat called her Chick-a-Dee.

The Piano

I had always been musical, and without power there I found myself really wanting a piano. I did not say anything about it because we had no money, so I prayed and asked God if I could have a piano. I told God that I would play hymns to Him on it as much as I could.

Not even a week went by and Pat came home one day and asked me if I wanted to go to an auction sale in town the next day. I said, "What are they selling?" and Pat said "There is everything you can think of, even a piano is going to be delivered there."

I could not believe my ears when he said Piano. I asked "Who's selling it?" he told me, and when I went to bed that night I asked God if he could not let the Piano be delivered to the auction site to give me a chance to approach the lady that owned it, and buy it privately because we had very little money. Maybe I could convince her to sell it to me cheaper than it would sell for at the auction.

The next day we got ready, all excited, and off to the auction sale. As we pulled into town we had to stop at the store, and the very first person we met going into the store was the woman who owned the piano. I was so excited I jumped out of the truck and went running up to her to ask if she was selling a piano at the auction. She said "Yes, I am, but for some reason the guys that were supposed to pick it up and deliver it to the auction did not come and it is still at my house."

I said "Can I buy it from you now instead of at the auction sale?" She said she guessed so. I asked how much she wanted for it and she replied "Oh, I don't know. Maybe fifty bucks."

I quickly handed her the $50 and thanked her and thanked God all the way home for answering my prayer.

We had it picked up and delivered to our house. It was a brass-back upright piano, very old and heavy, in excellent condition. I managed to find a professional tuner to come out where we lived to tune it in. I sanded all the paint off and varnished it to show the beautiful wood grain. I played hymns on it every chance I had.

A few months later, an old friend of my family who was a Pastor, drove all the way out to our place to visit us. I was very surprised because he lived 1000 miles away and took the time to come find us. I was telling him the story behind the piano and when he left, he threw $200 on the table and said, "God bought this Piano for you."

A Magic Moment

One of Pat's old friends came to visit us from Alberta. Pat wanted to take him out so we went to the bar because they had a Live Band playing there that night. The bar was just packed full, and it seemed everyone we knew was there.

The music started and they were very good. We all loved it. They had a dance floor in front of the band and everyone was dancing and really enjoying the good music.

Pat never danced in his life and when we got together he did bring himself to dance, just a short time, with me a couple times just fooling around.

Suddenly the band started to play "Storms Never Last" by Waylon Jennings and Jesse Colter. I really loved that song, and I jumped up and said "Pat, please dance with me for this song. I really love it"

He surprised me and jumped up and started to waltz with me. Him jumping up to dance caused all the people in the bar, which was packed full, to stop in their tracks. No one else got on the floor, they all stood and watched.

I think he surprised himself too because when he started to waltz, he blushed, which he did not often do. He stared into my eyes with the most tender look of love ever. I stared into his eyes too, and suddenly it was just like time stood still, and the world went away. There was just him and I, and no one else, just locked together in time. I knew he was feeling it too, it was absolutely magical. The whole bar of people felt it.

When the song was over, we went and sat down. There were people crying, watching us. People swarmed around our table saying how beautiful we looked. I even heard someone accusing another of being jealous.

We had many magic moments together, but this one seemed in front of the world.

The Explosion

One day, Pat and I went riding horses at my mom and dad's place. Pat was breaking-in a beautiful Pinto stallion, and it was about the third time it had ever been ridden. Things were going fine, and then all of a sudden the stallion started to panic and bucked him off. The worst of it was when Pat landed on the ground; the stallion kicked him with both feet.

By the time we got home to our place in Moberly Lake a few days later, Pat's whole side, from his ribs down to between his hip and knee, had turned black. There were no broken bones, but he could hardly move.

He said we should go to town the next day, and he would see a Doctor. I agreed, "I'll curl my hair then." We didn't have power where we lived, it was too far out in the bush, so I would pin-curl my hair.

Earlier that day a friend came to visit Pat and left him one homemade beer, which Pat set beside the bed.

So that night I propped a mirror on my night table, beside the kerosene lamp so I could talk with Pat while I curled my hair. It used to take a long time because my hair was long. It was so quiet, with no power out in the bush, the only sound was coming from us as we talked quietly. Also it was very dark, and my lamp was the only source of light in the house.

Suddenly "BANG!!!"

Sounding like a gunshot to me, and glass flying everywhere, I thought someone was shooting. I quickly blew out the lamp and hit the floor. In the darkness Pat pulled himself across the bed and said,

"Were you hit?!"

I said "Get down! Get down! He's shooting!"

Pat said "Who?"

I said "Jim!"

Jim was a little man that had been staying out there in another cabin, and was a bit 'off the wall' at times.

Pat said "No. That was not a gunshot, it sounded like something else. By then he was up on his feet and stumbled across the floor and found a flashlight. He started looking around and found glass all over the room. He looked where the bottle of beer had been and it was gone, blown to bits.

It took me a while to calm down from that because I had been so convinced that it was Jim shooting. I was afraid of the dark to begin with, so that made it worse. We laughed about this so many times over the years.

Signs of Pat's oncoming Death

I am not usually a superstitious person, but I do know there are certain unusual things that do have meaning. Here are a few of those things.

Native People's always said that the Eagle was the bearer of good news, and the Owl was the bearer of bad news.

A week before Pat's death, we were driving home in the early evening. It was dark because it was March, and it still got dark early that time of the year.

Suddenly, BANG! A huge white owl, wings widely spread, smashed into our windshield, covering the whole windshield with it's wingspan.

I screamed, Pat slowed down and stopped right away and got out. He looked around everywhere, and found nothing.

During that same week, we woke up one morning to a very loud blaring sound. It sounded like some kind of prehistoric monster. I jumped out of bed and went straight out on the balcony off our bedroom. The sound was coming straight towards our bedroom from something 100 yards away in the bush. It was so loud that it carried everywhere. I was frantic, and said "What is that?!"

Pat replied quietly "It's a cow moose." And he didn't even get out of bed, he just looked very somber. I looked it up on the internet a few months ago, to see if I could find that sound from a cow-moose. All the sounds that are from moose on internet that I found are not even close to that sound. So I looked up the sounds that a Sasquatch makes, and sure enough, I found exactly what we heard screaming at our bedroom that morning, and it was from a Sasquatch!

Two days before Pat died, he tried to wake me up in the night. He said "Come and get up with me to talk to me." I could barely hear him, I was in such a deep sleep. I couldn't get myself to get up. I could barely hear him pacing the floor.

The next night, the night before he died, I once again was only awake enough to see him slip his clothes on and go downstairs, to pace the floors again.

This was something I've always regretted, I wish I could have woke up enough to get up with him. I believe he must have been told his time was up somehow, I really believe that, because I caught him sitting and watching our children playing outside a few days before with tears running down his face. He did not tell me why when I hugged him and asked what was wrong. I thought he was just touched at the beauty of our children playing.

Pat's Sister's Gift

From the other side of the Veil

Two days before Pat passed away, his nephew had a vision/dream. His mother, Pat's sister who had passed away the year prior, met him at the doorway of a beautiful log building. He was holding his baby girl, and his mother said "Let me hold the baby, when you go in, walk around the table. Do not talk to anyone, and meet me back here."

He looked inside and saw Pat sitting and laughing with all the relations and friends who had passed on. His sister looked at her son and said "Now you know why I brought you here. It's Pat's time to leave, and there will be great devastation among the people when they hear."

He walked around the large table without a word said. His family members and friends that had passed away were all laughing and enjoying themselves. Pat was happy sitting among them.

He returned to the door where his mother stood waiting. She gave his baby back to him and said "When you go back you must be strong for the family, especially for Nellie or she might pass away before her time. When you go and see Nellie, she will be standing by herself, go and hug her."

So, he came to see me the day Pat was killed in the truck accident. I was standing by myself, beside the wood stove when he entered the house. He came over to me and hugged me, and held me. As soon as he hugged me, a powerful force came out of his chest and went into mine. Immediately I felt a total peace and calmness. He said to me "It was meant to be, it was his time." Then he told me what had happened and what was told to him when he was taken to the other side of the veil. The calmness gave me acceptance and washed away all doubts. It was so very beautiful, powerful and amazing. I said to him "Please stay close to me through all of this." He did. He really did get me through the horrible motions of the funeral week.

Now, to think back to what had happened, it is so wonderful to realize that Pat's sister sent the gift of Strength and Knowing, to me from the other side of the veil through her son. Today I feel very thankful and blessed that this wonderful thing happened in the middle of the worst thing that has ever happened to me.

The Night the Northern Lights

Came to see me

One night, after Pat had died, I was getting ready for bed. The night was very dark, and very still. We lived in a large log house on the other side of Moberly Lake and did not have power or running water, so there was no noise of any kind. The kids were all sleeping and as I was preparing for bed I was filled with such sadness I could hardly contain it. I thought, I will go out on the deck, outside our bedroom and pray with all my heart.

I stepped out on the deck and looked into the sky. I started to cry and pray. First I prayed to our Heavenly Father, and to Jesus Christ, and soon I was talking to Pat, his mom, my dad, and to all those I love on the other side.

My prayer became so strong, that I was throwing my voice out into the Heavens, and throwing myself out into the Heavens. All of this, without making a sound, so I would not wake the kids.

I cried out all my pain and sadness so very hard, and asked them to please help me.

Like I said, the sky was very dark, no light at all. I had seen one ray of a Northern Light flicker above me. Soon there was another one, and then another. Then many came, and all formed a perfect circle above me. The formation was huge and scared me so much, that I grabbed the door handle, but I did not go in. I stood and watched for a very long time. I knew they had all come to comfort me and to let me know that I was not alone. It was absolutely magnificent!

    I didn't want to go in the house because I knew in my heart that they would be gone as soon as I did. Finally, I told them I loved them, and that I was so thankful they all came and showed themselves to me. I thanked them over and over, and told them I had to go in.

    I opened the door, and slipped inside. I shut the door only for about ten seconds, and went out again to see if they were still there. They were not. In those ten seconds, everyone had disappeared. Not one flicker of light in the sky to be seen anywhere.

    Written June 28, 2015
    By Nellie Garbitt

Flowers from Heaven

One day a friend from church came to visit me and brought me a painted flower pot with a blooming pansy in it. It was a lovely gift and I really appreciated it.

A couple of days later, I looked out my front window and the lady across the street was chopping off all her big blooming Peonies. They were gorgeous and I was wondering why she was chopping them off, so I went across the street and asked her why she was doing that. She said "They're hanging down too much." I asked what she was going to do with them. She answered "Take them if you like, or I will be throwing them out."

So I took them home, all fifty of them. I put them in every vase, jar and jug I could find and surrounded myself with them. I felt special, my house smelt and looked so beautiful.

So the next day, my two daughters, a friend and I, decided we wanted to go and visit one of my sons in another town. So we packed overnight bags and left in the morning. As we drove, the girls were just talking and laughing together and enjoying the trip. I was happy and deep within my own thoughts. I was thinking, things do come in three's sometimes, and I have had flowers given to me two times in a row, so maybe there would be a third time. So I found myself praying as I was driving along, and I said "God, thank you for all the flowers that have been given to me. Sometimes it happens in three's, so if it could happen one more time, could it please happen this trip, and could it please be a rose. And could that rose please be from Pat to me." I went on to say, "It's ok God, if this does not happen, but thank you already if it does."

I did not tell anyone what I had prayed, it was my own little private conversation with God.

We arrived at my son's apartment, and as we were going up the stairs, there was a rosebush full of roses growing beside the stairs, and I thought, 'I bet someone will pick one for me,' but no, no one did. They all went out on the town, and I stayed at the apartment, and when they got back, our friend had a rose tucked behind her ear. I thought 'I bet she gives me that rose.' But no, she did not give me the rose. So I thought, 'Oh well, that's ok.' And I just put the thought away and enjoyed our visit.

We left, and on our way home we were driving through a town, and passed a big grocery store. Our friend said "You know, we should stop and buy groceries here, it is much cheaper." We had already passed it, so I turned around and drove into the parking lot. The girls said they did not want to come in, so I said it was ok, that I would do it and would hurry along.

By this time I had forgotten about the rose thing, and when I entered the store I saw a bunch of flowers including roses and thought, 'Well, it doesn't count if I buy a rose for myself, so it's ok, maybe I was just being silly to pray for that.'

I was at the back of the store, putting things in the cart when my daughter and our friend came walking up to me, my daughter holding twelve red roses and our friend holding twelve peach roses. At the same time they both said "Here mom. These are for you, you deserve them."

I was stunned, I said "You girls don't even know the great thing you are doing right now."

I told them about my prayers to God on our way the day before, and that they were really from Pat in Heaven. I could not stop thanking God and Pat all the way home. I felt as though I was walking on air.

I asked God for one rose from Pat, and I received twenty-four.

In the past I never really did have good luck with roses. When you buy rose buds, most of the time they would never open, and even if they opened a bit, they always died in a week or so. Well, these roses were unbelievable. They all opened, really wide, and they did not die off for three weeks.

I have included a real picture of them, I took quite a few because they were so special and stayed so long, and because they really were, Flowers from Heaven, and proves that God really does answer all Prayers, even if they seem silly.

The Morning Jesus Spoke to me

I woke up at exactly 5:30. I got up and went to the table to read, and to pray. Like I did many mornings. As I prayed, I started to cry, saying to God, 'Please help me not to make another mistake. If I do this. I just want to do your Will.' I had cleaned up my life, got Baptized, quit smoking, quit anything that I thought was wrong. I had to make the decision to marry instead of living together, and I was afraid.

A voice came to me on my right shoulder. I could see a beautiful, masculine, tanned arm reach outwards and bent as if for me to link mine into His and He said "Come I will lead the way." His Love was pouring down on me so strong that I thought, he loves me more than anyone in the world, and I will not tell anyone that he loves me the most. The room was filled with Him and His Love.

Slowly he started to withdraw. I knew he had to, or there would be nothing that I would want in this world than to be with Him.

It was the most powerful thing that has ever happened to me in my life.

The 1st Time I was shown

A little bit of Heaven

During one time when I had moved, I was packing things into the building I was moving into, and an acquaintance that was living in the building too offered help to take care of my bird and cage until I was settled, so I agreed. Once I was moved in, I said to the friend "Could I have my bird back now?"

She answered with "No, it is my bird."

I was quite ticked off about this and could not understand how someone could claim something that was not theirs.

It was before suppertime and I thought I would lie down on the bed for a while. This was very unusual for me to ever go and lay down in bed at this time of day. As soon as a laid down, I fell right to sleep.

Right away I was taken to a most beautiful place. I don't know who was taking me there because he stood behind my left shoulder, and I did not look. This place had birds and flowers, and they were the most beautiful birds I had ever seen. Nothing like any birds I have seen on this earth. The colors and shapes of them were unbelievable. I looked and one of the birds was loving a red rose. They were loving each other so much that they would kind of dissolve into one another, and then come apart, and then go back, and come apart again. These birds had beautiful long fan tails that hung down in such a beautiful way. I was in awe.

Then, all of a sudden, I could hear two women's voices, and one said to the other "What's she doing here?"

I looked sideways to my right, and there were two little birds sitting in a big nest of Forget-me-Not flowers.

Just then, I started to hear the most beautiful tones I have ever heard. They were like beautiful, deep, rich, living tones. There are no words here on earth to properly describe what those tones sound like, but they were more beautiful than any tone you could imagine.

Betty Eadie, in her book "The Awakening Heart" heard those tones and tried to explain what they sounded like too. I only started to hear them, and immediately I was awakened. I got up and sat at the table, and as clear as a bell, the words came to me "Keep your treasures in Heaven, for everything on earth will pass away and return to dust."

I thought to let the woman have the bird, it is the good and right thing to do. It made me think, not to be too attached to things on earth because what we have waiting for us on the other side is so much more beautiful. It made me think, 'how do I build my treasures in Heaven?' and also, what can we take with us when we leave… just the love and goodness we feel and do for one another and for God.

The 2ⁿᵈ time I was shown Heaven

I was taken to the other side of the veil in a dream. I do not know who it was that took me there. He was off to my left side, and behind me enough so I could not see. I did not even try to see who he was.

We crossed over, and what I saw was a big multitude of people, and in front of them was a man talking to them, and teaching them.

My Guide said to me, "That is the Apostle Peter." As soon as Peter saw us, he walked right over to us and started to talk to me. It seemed like the most natural thing in the world for me to be talking to the Apostle Peter. I do not remember what was said, but somehow I feel it had something to do with my journey.

At that time, I honestly did not know that Peter was called an Apostle. I thought he was called a Disciple. It was not until quite a while later that I learned Peter is called Apostle Peter, and not Peter the Disciple.

Angels wake me to Pray

I was waking up at exactly 5:30 every morning. After I joined the church I would wake up, then get up and read the Bible a little, then pray and go back to bed.

Sometimes I would hear my name being called, "Nellie, Nellie..." sometimes it would be a woman's voice, and sometimes it would be a man's. I would get up, it would always be 5:30. So I would read, and pray, and go back to bed.

Sometimes I would hear the phone ringing and wake up. I'd get up, the phone would not be ringing, so I'd look at the clock, it was always 5:30, so I would pray and read.

Other times I would hear someone knocking at the door. I would get up, and no one was knocking, I would look at the clock and once again, 5:30. Again I would go read the Bible, pray, and go back to bed.

So really, this can happen to us all if we faithfully get up, read the Bible, and pray early in the morning.

Four things told to me by God

Long after Pat had passed away, I was in another relationship with a man I had known for a few years. During that relationship, he cheated on me with another woman. This left me with a weird, kind of ugly, sick feeling in my stomach that stayed for about a year.

I was visiting with my good friend one day and said to her "I wonder how to get rid of this feeling?" she said "I don't know." So that next morning I got up and sat at my table and prayed with all of my heart to God and talked to him about this feeling. I was crying and asking him what to do. Instantly a male voice said to me;

- "Faith, the size of a mustard seed can move a mountain."

Right away I said in return, "What has that got to do with this feeling I have in my stomach?" his answer came back right away saying,

- "Faith is a gift of God, you have to ask for it."

That just bewildered me, because I thought you had to try and have Faith and acquire Faith in God on our own through life. Then he said,

- "Believe in your own prayers."

Again, I was bewildered. All of my life I thought people with strong Faith had the strongest prayers, and periodically I would ask for prayers to help ease the pain and problems I was having. The next thing he said was,

- "Pray for her, every time you see her, pray with all your heart for her." While he was saying this I could clearly see her crying, with her head on my chest, and me hugging her.

I was so excited about God coming and answering me so clearly that I could hear him, that I grabbed a piece of paper and pen, and wrote every word down so I would never forget.

Well, 'Her', meaning the lady that he had cheated on me with. I hardly ever saw her before that day I prayed, but after that I would see her every time I would leave my house for about six months. I would pray for her every time.

The wonderful thing about this is, after I had prayed for her about three times, that feeling in my stomach was gone. It was completely gone, and I had compassion for her.

So now, a year later, she ended up with this man, and I was starting to see someone else. We happen to meet each other in another town, in a public place, and we started to talk about the situation right away. I said "Let's go to the bathroom so we can talk privately." Once we entered the bathroom, she started to be very angry and was saying nasty things. I said "I was mad at you too, but listen to what I have to say…" So she listened while I told her that God told me to pray for her every time I would see her, and I told her I did, and still was. She burst out crying and came and put her head on my chest, and I held her.

So God gave me confirmation. That is really was Him that told me the four things while I was praying that day. By having her cry on my chest and me holding her just like I had seen while God told me to pray for her.

My Daughter Willow's Birth

Foretold by an Angel

Two years after Pat passed to the other side, I was so lonely and started a relationship with my daughter Willow's father.

I did not plan to have any more children, as I was forty-four years old at the time.

One morning, just as I was waking, I dreamt or had a vision that I was lying on my back, and the sky was so beautifully-blue above me. A bald headed eagle was flying over me and a beam of light from beside the eagle shot down straight into my uterus.

Then about a week later, I dreamt I had milk running out of both my breasts. Again another week later, I had that same dream.

Then, a month later, a dream/vision came that was definitely from the other side of the veil.

What looked to me to be a Wise Man, dressed in white up to his head-covering, stood not too far from me. His surroundings seemed to exude Wisdom. He said to me "Nellie, you are going to have another baby, but don't worry about anything, because everything will be alright."

I went to the Doctor when my monthly time didn't come. He told me I was indeed pregnant, and because of my age, he would give me the option of abortion. I said, No. He wanted to take out some amniotic fluid to test for abnormalities, and again, I said No.

When I went for an ultrasound, at about four months, the technician said "What is this?"

I looked and there was a light, right on the baby's head. She said, "I have never seen this, please wait while I go get a specialist to come look."

When the specialist saw the light, he said "I have never seen anything like this either, there is nothing to make anything reflect light in there. I want you to come back in two weeks for another ultrasound."

So in two weeks I went back, but there was no light showing this time. I knew right away when I saw the light on her head what it was. Spirits sometimes look like little sparks of light to our normal eye. When I saw it I knew that they, her guardian spirits, were showing me that they are with her and for me not to worry.

Eagle Feathers

During my pregnancy with Willow, her father and I both had dreams about eagle feathers at the same time. I dreamt that there was an eagle flying right over my head and almost touched me. It was coming out of a nest-like place that looked like it was built in a beaver dam. I was reaching out trying to pull a couple of feathers, but I couldn't grasp them. I said to the eagle, "Can I just have a couple of your feathers?"

The eagle looked back at me, and kept flying away. I looked down at the nest it came out of and there, lying side by side, were two beautiful, long eagle feathers left behind for me.

The same morning Willow's father woke up and told me he had a dream that he had to go find two eagle feathers to give me for the baby. He went out into the bush and came back that night with two, long, beautiful eagle feathers, and gave them to me.

Willow Napoleon

Willow Napoleon

An Angel Sent to Us

Have you ever wondered why there are people who are born mentally handicapped? I sure did. The answer came to me in a few different ways to help me explain this.

I have had the privilege of getting to know, and be a part of an Angel's life. She is Patsy Garbitt, Pat's first daughter with his first wife. Patsy was born mentally handicapped. In the Native communities, in the 1950's and 60's, the government, Ministry of Children and Families, went around and collected all the children who were mentally handicapped, and they Institutionalized them. The Ministry didn't encourage communication, and many of these native children were lost in the process.

In the 1980's, the government closed down these institutions, and moved all the patients to Care-Homes. We were lucky enough to find Patsy.

Pat told me, when I first met him, that he had a hurt that could never be fixed, and would suffer and carry the memory of Patsy with him for the rest of his life. That always bothered me, I wished I could have helped in some way.

Once day we were visiting in Fort St. John. I was moved so strongly to call one of these Care-

Homes in the hopes that I could find any information on where Patsy could have ended up.

Well, as soon as I started to speak with the Care Aid, and mentioned Patsy's name, she began to cry. I said "Why are you crying?" and the lady replied "Patsy is right here! We thought she was one of the lost ones and didn't know if we'd ever find her family!"

So immediately I went to the Care Home to see her. Pat could not bring himself to come with me, all he could do was cry. I told him not to worry, that everything would be ok, and I left to see her. By the time I got there, I was so afraid, and before I walked into the building, I stood and prayed, and asked God for help.

After the Care Aid and I cried with Patsy sitting beside her, I started to talk about her family. Everything I could say that may help her I said. Patsy reacted immediately, letting us know that she, in some way, could understand as she could not speak. It was a miracle.

The second time I went to visit, sometime later, I sat on the couch when Patsy came and sat beside me on her own. They gave her a glass of juice to drink, she handed it to me. I took a drink and handed it back to her, then she took a drink, and handed it back to me. She then laid her head on my shoulder. Again the Care Aid cried and said Patsy had never done anything like that before.

I left with my cup overflowing, crying and thanking God. Pat cried, but he was relieved to finally know how she was doing.

Then the day came when Pat got brave enough to come with me. He brought twelve roses, and when he entered the room and went to her, she hollered, waiving her arms. Letting us all know that she knew him. The next time Pat went with me, he sat on the couch and spoke Cree to her. Another time when he was sitting in the vehicle with her, Patsy put her hand on Pat's knee.

Finally, they could start healing from the years spent apart, and Pat's heart started to mend.

What I learned
From Handicapped People

After Pat's death, I read Betty Edie's books. Her second book entitled 'The Awakening Heart', told about why people come to earth handicapped. She said that she was shown on the other side that the spirits that chose to come here that way are our teachings. They are Mighty Spirits that chose to come here in that way to teach us how to love one another. Coming to earth in an uncomely body, or other challenges, sometimes makes it harder to love, and this is the exact factor that our hearts become soft, and loving to help them, and love them.

I dreamt a dream of Patsy one time. In the dream, the world was in chaos. I was trying to help her lay down on a cot because she was sick. As I was waking up from this dream I could hear "Anything you do to one of these, you do straight unto me."

It was Jesus.

So considering what Christ said, it is a huge privilege to have one of these special spirits in your presence. Always remember, when you help them, you are helping Christ himself.

My Dreams of Pat

I have dreamt of Pat many times since the day he left. Here are just a few:

* I dreamt Pat and I were playing together, flying up and down walls, having a lot of fun.

* I dreamt he came to me and I could see very clearly in the dream, that he had not left me, he was in my subconscious.

* I dreamt of him twice in a row, in the space of an hour. It was after I had my tubes tied, and I was in a lot of pain. It was hard to sleep or even turn in my bed. I fell asleep and there, was Pat. He was walking in the house and I was so excited to see him. I said "You're not dead, everyone thinks you are dead." I burst out crying saying "I love you Pat! I Love you Pat! he told me "I love you too, but don't cry anymore."

"I don't want to cry anymore," I said to him. "I have a baby, and have been with others…"

He told me he knew, and he didn't seem concerned at all. Then I said "I love you." And I started to cry again, then he was gone. I made my way out of the bed, in much pain, and sat at the table thinking of how clear and certain I knew he came to visit. I was angry at myself for crying, thinking that had sent him away.

I went back to bed, and as soon as I fell asleep, there he was again. This time I made sure I did not cry. I said to him "Why are you here?"

He responded with "I cannot tell you that."

I asked "When are you going back?"

His answer; "I am not going back."

Then I looked into his eyes and said "Why are you here? Are you helping Jesus because the end is coming soon?"

We were talking… but our mouths were not moving. Then he walked away.

We are One

I prayed and asked God if he could tell Pat for me that I love him more than I ever did, and that we are one.

About three months later, I was coming out of my sleep, and the Lord brought me to Pat so I could tell him myself. I told him, and then thought, 'Wow, how great this is that God has answered this prayer in the most perfect way.' Making me so grateful.

Answer to Prayer

Years after Pat's death, I would occasionally have a disturbing dream that he had been away from me all these years, and did not come to see me because he was with someone else.

I told my friend about this over the phone, and said "I wonder why I dream this kind of dream, it always upsets me."

"Let's both pray and ask God what this means." She replied. So we both prayed that night about it. The next morning she called me very excited, she asked "Do you have some kind of old dresser? Like an antique?" I said in fact I did. She had not been to my house for a few years.

This was the dream she was given after praying that night:

* She said she had seen Pat's pictures, like a collage on this old dresser. There were twelve black Clydesdales running off the side of it. The Clydesdales were pulling a carriage with Pat and I in it. Pat and I were so close, we were blending into one another, as we were one, looking very beautiful together.

She didn't know that Pat's favorite horses were black Clydesdales, and that Pat told me when he was still here with me that he and I, are 'One'.

I did have a collage of Pat's pictures against the mirror on that old dresser.

I never had that dream again

Pat's Extraordinary Experiences

Pat had many experiences, some already written in these pages, many that will not be written. Here are a few stories I thought worth sharing, just to prove that many things are possible...

*When Pat was a young man, he was walking up the little hill at the beginning of Boucher Lake Road. As he was walking, he looked sideways and saw a Fairy flying along beside him. He said it looked just like the Walt Disney Fairy. He said she just flew along beside him. He was afraid to tell anyone because he thought no one would believe him.

*One hunting trip, Pat was guiding a hunter from the United States. They were hunting up in the mountains of Northern British Columbia, in the Gataga River country. Pat and his Hunter were taking a break on the top of a mountain. They looked at the mountain closest to them, and there, on the top of the peak, was a Sasquatch. It was sunning itself, laying there with its' hands behind it's head. They watched it for a long time, using binoculars to have a good look. They didn't have a camera with them.

The Sasquatch looked tall, with long hair just like any reference pictures show. Then it stood up and walked around the other side of the mountain.

Pat and his Hunter journeyed down their mountain, and up the next, to where the Sasquatch was seen. It had clouded over and started to snow by the time they were half way up the mountain. By the time they reached the top, the ground was covered with snow, and the Sasquatch was out of site. They regretted not having a camera with them.

*Pat was on horseback coming back from Fort Nelson to Moberly Lake. He was riding through the mountains down the Alaska Highway because he was coming back from doing Geological surveys. As he travelled from one mountain to another, his horse became tired because it was heavily packed, so Pat walked beside it. He became very tired, but didn't stop. As he was reaching each mountain he would look up, and in the blink of an eye, somehow he was on the next mountain!

He said he didn't know how he got there, but it kept happening from one mountain to the next. Somehow he was 'carried' from one, to the next.

*I woke up during the night once, with Pat saying "Did you see it? Did you see it?!"

I asked "See what?"

He said "There was a big light that came in our room. It had so much Love!" by then he had tears rolling down his face. He said it was a Beautiful Light.

*One day, long after Pat's brother Slim had passed, Pat drove into the driveway of the piece of land he owned on the other side of Moberly Lake. It was before anyone lived there. When he arrived, there, standing as clear as could be, was his brother Slim. Pat said they talked together for a long time, and then Slim left. I wonder to this day why I didn't ask him what they spoke about, but at that time, I felt out of Respect not to.

*When Pat's nephew Eddy died, Pat was far out in the bush, camping. During the night he said Eddy had come into his tent and said his goodbyes, and left. The next morning, when people came to get Pat, to tell him what happened, Pat was dressed and waiting for them. He told them he already knew why they were coming to get him

*Pat had many dreams that also came true.

Nell's Extraordinary Experiences

  Here are just a few experiences that have happened to me over the years. I thought they are worth mentioning, with hopes they may bring someone even a small bit of inspiration.

  *After Pat's death, someone gave me a book to read that changed the way I looked at things forever. This book was called 'Embraced by the Light' by Betty Eadie. It was the first Christmas without Pat, and my children and I were very lonely and sad.

  Each night when I went to bed, I would take this book and read a few pages. It lifted my spirits every time I would pick it up. One of those nights, I was reading it and I heard wings fluttering around me while I lay there reading. I knew it was an Angel, come to comfort me.

  *After I joined the Church, a lot of things would happen to me. People that I knew had passed away, would come to me in dreams. They would never speak to me, and they always looked beautiful.

  *Also after joining, I was taking a nap on the couch one day, and as I woke up, I realized I was above my body. I thought, 'This feels nice, I wonder how I go back?' So I thought about going into my body, and immediately I was back in. Then, I thought 'Can I do this again?' so I gave a little push, and out I came again only closer to my body than the first time. Then, I thought I would go back in again, and I did. So, a third time, I thought, 'I will try one more time, and then I will not do it again…' so I did, and this time I barely lifted out, so I made myself go back in.

I wondered why this happened to me. In the past, I had a friend who could do this, and I told her I didn't want to know how. I forgot about this for a year or so, then one day I woke up to that feeling again. I thought 'Should I try this again?' so I did, and as soon as I started to lift out, I stopped it, and didn't try it again. I didn't understand this, and just left it alone. If nothing else, this does prove that we do have a Body, and we do have a Spirit, and when the Body dies… the Spirit lives on.

*When I was going through a very rough period of about a year, I really could feel and see my Spirit Guide. He would come to me at least four times a day. He was a native man, with braids. I could never see his eyes, but always felt his face close to mine. He was wise and kind, and he seemed a normal part of my life at the time. Guides may be different beings from time to time, depending on what we need.

*I had spent the winter in Southern British Columbia, and was going through rough times. I decided to leave and go back home. I told my friend, and she said "I'll drive back with you and the kids." So I packed up and by the time we left, it was getting dark and was snowing very hard.

We made it about one hour out of town and decided to get a room because it was snowing so hard. During the night, we talked and talked, and I decided to go back and stay a couple more weeks before making the trek home. When morning came I took my truck into the garage because it had started to make a small noise

The mechanic came out to talk to me and was shaking his head. He said "You must have someone taking care of you lady."

I asked why, and he continued "There is nothing holding your drive shaft in this truck. I don't understand how you drove this truck in here."

Once again… proof that we really are being looked after.

*Pat used to tell me stories about his life as we travelled together. Sometimes I would get so excited about the outcome of the story, I would interrupt him before the story was finished. He didn't like it when I would cut him off in conversation, so when I did this, he wouldn't finish the story.

One night we were driving up the hill coming out of Hudson's Hope going to Moberly Lake, and he was telling me a story. I thought he was driving kind of fast, it was night time, and the roads were snowy, but I sat back and listened.

As we climbed the hill, I started to get 'that' feeling in my stomach. With this feeling, my mind kept saying 'Moose. Moose.' I kept quiet because I didn't want to interrupt so I could hear the end of the story. As we drove along, that feeling got stronger, and stronger, while the voice saying 'Moose! MOOSE!' was getting louder and louder..

Finally I screamed "MOOSE!"

Pat slammed on his brakes and a huge bull moose jumped out in front of our truck! We didn't hit it.

Pat asked "How did you do that? If I had not stepped on the brake, we would have hit it!"

*It was after Pat's death, my daughter Rosalee (Chickadee) and I had gone to my mom's for a visit. On the way home, an Eagle flew in front of our truck and landed in the middle of the road, right in front of us only about ten feet away. It was a huge Golden Eagle. It stayed there, and looked at us for a very long time. We needed to go home so we moved forward until it flew up on a fence post right beside up, and it stayed there. We finally drove away and left it. I always wondered what that was about…

*One time, there were two ladies that died in Chetwynd, one had worked in the bank for twenty years, and the other was the daughter of one of the Doctors in town. I went to bed thinking of how it says in the Bible how God can use us to do his Will. It said we can be simulated like being Fine China, or we could be like a container that holds garbage. Both are needed, but being used as Fine China would be better.

I was thinking of how these ladies had an important role in life. As soon as I thought that, a voice came to me and said "Nellie, you have an important role too."

It made me feel so good, and it made me realize that each one of us have an important role in this lifetime, whether you believe it or not. Each one of us are needed to complete our Missions, and help others to complete theirs. Our life is like a book, with chapters beginning, and chapters ending. If you really look back, you can see where once ended, and a new one started.

*I did see the Moberly Lake Monster, along with two other ladies. It looked about forty or fifty feet long, with an eel-like body. It was stuck where the water is shallow at West Moberly First Nations.

Cleansed our Home of all Evil

I wanted to include this story in the book, to let people know that you really can protect yourself from all evil. It is a story of what I did one time, when everything in my home was unsettled. There was no peace, and arguments were daily.

I was sitting at the table one day pondering about why my family were not getting along, and there seemed to be no peace in our home. Then it hit me, as clear as can be, there was a lot of drinking amongst some of the family members, causing trouble. I realized, without a doubt, that we needed prayer over us and our house. I had heard many times in my life that people would get someone to pray over them and their home. I decided right then that I would do this. I planned to go out on the road in front of my house, and pray over it, and everyone in it.

It was just getting dark, and the night air was cool. I slipped on a sweater and headed for the door. By the time I got to the door, my teeth were chattering. I snuggled the sweater around me tighter, and walked out to the road. When I reached the road, my teeth were chattering so hard I couldn't have talked, and my body was shaking so hard, as if I were freezing. I thought 'I don't care how bad this shaking is, I'm doing this anyway.'

I started to pray. This is exactly what I said and what happened:

"Heavenly Father, I come to you in the name of your son, Jesus Christ. I ask if you could please wash my house, and everything, and everyone in it with the precious blood of your son, Jesus Christ.:

As soon as I said that, Bang, something hit my chest gently, and my whole body went from shaking very hard, to absolutely still and peaceful.

I couldn't believe how quickly and wonderfully that happened. I thanked God our Father, and Jesus Christ our Savior very much for answering my prayer.

Peace returned to our home immediately after that prayer. Everyone got along really well again, and we were all happy.

This is proof that this kind of prayer works when you think evil is bothering you, or your family, friends or your Home.

My Testimony
Of a Priesthood Blessing

Two Missionaries from the Mormon Church stopped by to visit me one day. From the day I joined this Church my life changed, and I've had many wonderful spiritual experiences happen to me.

When they were ready to leave they asked if they could do anything for me. I said "Yes, could you pray over me and ask God to heal the ulcerated veins I have in my legs?"

For the previous year, I would get veins that would ulcerate, sometimes three or four at a time. They would take at least one month to heal and go away. By the time they would be gone, another two or three would form. They were painful, and the Doctor's said there was nothing they could do but watch them to make sure they didn't get too large, or put me in danger in any way.

So the Missionaries proceeded to pray over me. They called it giving me a 'Priesthood Blessing'. They put a touch of oil on my head, and both laid their hands on top of my head, and started to pray. During this Blessing, three times they said I was to listen to my Doctor. So when they were done and left, I thought I'd better go to the Dr, he must have help for these ulcers on my legs.

A couple of days later I made a trip in to the Dr. concerning the ulcers. During the visit he asked me if I was taking my medication properly for my Epilepsy, which was three pills a day. I told him I was only taking one or two a day because I had not had a seizure for seven years. Over the duration of the appointment, the Doctor repeated three times to take my Epilepsy medication properly. Each time I would say "I'm here for you to look at the ulcers on my legs."

The Dr. responded again with "We can only keep an eye on those ulcers, but you must take your other medication properly."

I left his office thinking 'I hadn't had a seizure in seven years! So I'm not going to increase that medication.'

So… three days later, I had a major seizure. 'WOW!' I thought 'I should have listened to the Missionaries when they said to listen to my Dr.!' Not only that, the ulcers on my legs disappeared in three days, and never returned.

This is true, and my Testimony of what the Church calls "Priesthood Blessings", and how they really work when you need help.

Seeing 11:11

I have seen the numbers 11:11 daily on the clock for years now. Each night when I prepare to go to bed, I see this number when I look at the clock. I never plan to go to bed at a certain time, and I don't always look at the clock at the same time when I go to bed. Sometimes I will look at the clock when I enter the bedroom and it will be 11:11. Or sometimes I won't think of looking at the clock until I am in bed and almost asleep, then I look and it's 11:11. This has been happening to me for many years now, and I never could figure it out.

There is a lot on the internet about this now. Some articles say it is a new awakening, while others say it is a sign of Twin Spirits.

I believe in my case, it would be the sign of Pat and I being Twin Spirits. Reminding me daily that he loves me, and he is still with me. Especially at bedtime, when I feel lonely, this comforts me.

11:11

Four Leaf Clovers

From the time that I was a little girl, for some reason I would always find four leaf clovers. I remember sitting beside the sandbox in a clover patch, and they would just jump out at me. I would pray and make a wish each time I would pick one.

As I got older, in my twenties and living out on my parent's farm, I would walk down to the cow pasture to milk the cows with my brothers. On the way back I would have clovers jumping out at me all the way. Sometimes I would have as many as fifteen or twenty 4-leaf clovers at a time. I would put them in water, or dry them in books. Almost every book would have a clover falling out of it years later.

At the farm our garden patch was next to the cow pasture. At times I would go down and work in the garden by myself. I would sit in the garden and sing the song "In the Garden". The words blow me away every time, and still do. My favorite being the part that says;

'I come to the garden alone, while the dew is still on the roses, and the voice I hear, falling on my ear, the Son of God discloses. And He walks with me, and He talks with me, and He tells me I am his own. And the joy we share, as

we tarry there, none other, has ever known. He speaks, and the sound of His voice, is so sweet, the birds hush their singing, and the melody that He gave to me, within my heart is ringing.'

Then on the way home, once again, I would find four leaf clovers jumping out, all the way back to the house.

This always made me feel special, and it was a private thing between myself and God it seemed. I thought this story was worthy of mentioning because I believe it is those beautiful, private moments, those communications with God, that He shows Himself to us. Then, we can know without a doubt, that He lives. No one can take that away from you. The world cannot take it away. It is yours to keep.

Pat Appeared

After Pat's death, he appeared to a friend of mine. When he died, she kept saying to him "Pat, if there is a Heaven, please show me so I can believe… but don't come up close to me and scare me."

She got up during the night, to grab something to eat. She happened to look out her window in the direction of my house, and there he was. She said he was all lit up and sitting in the living room of our house. She said she could look right through the wall of the house to see him sitting there.

She believed, after that.

My Last Words to Pat

When Pat was leaving that morning, we were hugging so many times. It seemed unusual and it made my daughter Chickadee cry. She would not let her daddy go. Finally when he was leaving I said to him "*Just remember the number 5.*" Chickadee and I waved at him from the big window until he was out of sight.

We had a boarder that had lived with us for many years. Pat came to him after he died and said to "Take Nellie to this place, behind one of the cabins, out in the bush. Tell her every time she needs strength to go there."

The first time I went there, while I was crying, there were *5 Eagles* circling above me high in the sky.

To Hear Pat's Voice Again

From the day Pat left me, I always watched and listened for him. I thought in some way he would come to me and talk to me, just like his mother after she passed used to talk to him when he would lay down to sleep at night.

I would try to feel him around me, and would just cry because I never could. He did come to me in many dreams though, so I relaxed with all that and accepted the blessings of the dreams I would have of him, when they came.

I had to be the Mother, and Father to our children after he was gone. Through the years it was tough and I always had to work to keep things going.

It was April 2015, twenty-two years after Pat died. I got home from work, so exhausted I could hardly think as usual. I walked to the fridge to get a plate of supper I had saved from our Easter dinner. As I took it out and walked towards the counter, Pat's voice said "I love you sweetheart." In Cree language. I was absolutely stunned. I sat down, taking in what had just happened. I said to Pat "It took me 22 years to hear you. Thank you so much for telling me you love me out loud so I can hear you." I shook my head and laughed thinking how stupid I had been all these years, because when he was alive with me, he always told me he loved me, but it was always in the Cree language.

    This is proof that we are always connected to our loved ones. I know they are busy doing things and learning on the other side too, but when something like this happens, it is such a huge blessing, and brings so much happiness!

To Face your Fears

One of my biggest fears my whole life, was to be left alone. I did have good reason for feeling this way because of the Epilepsy, and living out in the bush without power, running water or sewer, and only wood heating. These were all things I couldn't handle on my own. Also, in the winter the road would become impossible to travel on, and would leave me with my three children, stranded.

The pain of losing Pat was too unbearable for me to go through alone, I really needed someone with me deal with the loneliness and the feeling of helplessness of taking care of the children alone.

So I chose to try and find another man, to live with me and help me to survive. The choices I made were not right for me, or my children, and we all suffered because of these choices. Over and over I tried, but each time I realized the choice was wrong, and the effect it had on my children and I made me full of regret.

It took me fifteen years after Pat died, to finally face my fear of being alone, and just surrender to God with my life, and everything in it. Loneliness is like a monster in itself. It takes time and patience to tame this monster. I started to love myself and find out who I was again. I had lost my identity when Pat left, and I always felt I needed another man with me to make me feel grounded, and worthy of Love.

I became independent, and learned to love who I had become. God and my children became my main focus. I became confident in my working skills and became a Consultant. I started doing my artwork, and writing two books that can be left to my children, as well as those that will read them

Another thing happened that changed my life at the age of 61. My sister-in-law passed away very suddenly. It made me realize that I need to spend my time with things that mean a lot to me, because as a person gets older, we need to be doing the things that will mean something in the end. So that is what I am doing now, and loving it. It is not always smooth-sailing, but, in the end we all would like to leave some kind of Legacy. Something that means a lot, on this side of the veil, as well as the other.

My Reiki Treatment

I was taught Reiki, Level one, by a Reiki Master many years ago but I have never used it. My oldest daughter talked me into going for a Reiki treatment. Even with taking Level One, I wasn't really familiar with how Reiki treatments can work.

This is just a small part of the treatment given to me on August 01, 2016. This lady, that Treated me, communicated with my loved ones right from the beginning. She spoke of what she was getting from them for the two-hour long visit. I was very surprised at all of it:

*Pat came through quickly, a very strong presence, a man who loved the mountains and horses. She said he is working with horses now too. Pat told her 'This is my Woman", Pat always called me ('His Woman', he was a rough talker, and it sounded very endearing when he would introduce me this way) He said "This is my Woman" three times during the treatment.

*She said "He says you are a Lady, and he loves that about you. He says you have the old-way, and you know the old-way. He says society does not have this anymore and needs it. He says the old way he lived is not being followed by anyone anymore."

*She told me I was a young spirit, kind and generous, spiritual, and very connected to the God Head.

*She told me I was Native in a past life.

*Pat came through again and said "She is my Woman, and I did not, and do not have anyone else (another woman)

*Pat always used to tease me about how easily I would replace him if he died before me. So the next thing he says during my treatment was "You couldn't replace me could you?"

*Pat said "The kids need to read, they need to read, and they need to get out and do something. Not stay in the house all the time."

*She said "He's comical isn't he?" Pat was very comical all the time, he always made me laugh.

*She said "You read a lot." I told her I was writing a book and she told me "Pat says get used to travelling, you will be talking to a lot of people about your book."

*Then she told me "Your children are going to be doing really good."

This is only part of the reading she gave me, but I thought it was nice to mention. After all, it has been twenty two years since Pat's been gone, and it shows how connected we are still.

Pat's Funeral Announcement

Father of many, Uncle to all
Brother, Grandfather, Friend
We gather today to bid our farewells
While the Grandfathers echo your Name
Man of honor, Man of strength
And always a man of your word
Larger than life, you filled our lives
With the will to live strong and free
Strong spirited man with always a smile
You gave us a wonderful gift\The sound of Your laughter will always ring true
In our hearts, like a song in the wind.
Oh man of the mountains, the lakes and the trees
With your loved ones you will always be
Your journey's begun to your home in the sky
You're at Home now, at rest, at peace.

A Whisper from God

"I wait in many a heart, but few retire into that inner place of being to commune with me. Where ever the soul is, I am. Man has rarely understood this. I am actually at the center of every man's being, but, distracted with the things of the sense-life... he finds me not."

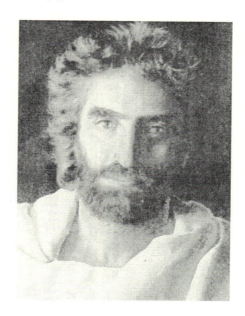

References

Betty Eadie *The Awakening Heart* 1996 a "roadmap" for healing, for overcoming adversity, anxiety and heart ache. It can build one's faith and trust in the Lord, and help them internalize their spiritual knowledge, thus building their faith into action in their daily life."

Betty Eadie *Embraced by the Light* 1992" I give the account of my near-death experience, having been told by Jesus that I had died and that it was "not yet" my time.

Keirsten White *The Chao of Stars* 2013 Kiersten White, New York Times bestselling author of Paranormalcy, is back with The Chaos of Stars, an enchanting novel set in Egypt and San Diego that captures the magic of first love and the eternally complicated truth about family.

Waylon Jennings *Storms Never Last* 1980 ALBUM Music Man

Nellie Garbitt *True Stories of Pat and Nell* 2017 British Columbia, Canada

Glossary

Eagle: Northeastern, British Columbia: *Totem Divine spirit, sacrifice, connection to creator, intelligence, renewal, courage, illumination of spirit, healing, creation, freedom, and risk-taker.*

Owl: Northeastern British Columbia: *Totem Wisdom, deception, intuition, insight, messenger, mystery, freedom, secrets, stealth, vision.*

Sasquatch: In American folklore, *Bigfoot (also known as Sasquatch) is a simian-like creature[2] that is said to inhabit forests, mainly in the Pacific Northwest. Bigfoot is usually described as a large, hairy, bipedal humanoid. The term sasquatch is an Anglicized derivative of the Halkomelem word sásq'ets*